high on a hill

A Book of Chinese Riddles

high on a hill

A Book of Chinese Riddles

Selected and Illustrated by ED YOUNG

COLLINS
New York and Cleveland

Library of Congress Cataloging in Publication
information may be found on last page of this book.

This book represents the cooperation of my entire family,
who collected the original material in China;
and also the special help of Fifi and Cathy Chou,
in whose hands it took form in English.

E.Y.

Summer maiden, all alight,
She's white
At night;
Turns dark, then bright.

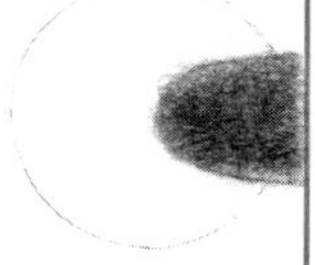

有位夏家姑娘
電燈裝在身上
夜裏出來白相
燈光一暗一亮

firefly

They love to work, although they're small,
And never, ever shirk at all;
They're gath'ring food, for winter's coming,
And, as they work, just hear them humming!

小小身體愛勞動
團結互助同做工
花兒開處嗡嗡叫
運回糧食好過冬

bees

Here's a pretty fellow
With wings just like a fairy,
Green jacket, red cap—
But oh! his legs are hairy!

背上生翅膀　頭戴紅纓帽
脚上長滿毛　身穿綠羅袍

fly

In gray fur coat, he looks quite sly
With pointed nose and beady eye.
This fellow sleeps when it is light
And steals and loots throughout the night.

灰先生身穿皮
鼻尖尖眼如葡
白天躲着睡覺袄
黑夜出來偷盜萄

mouse

He has a point at either end;
He looks too fierce to be a friend.
You'll see him the whole year around
Crawling slowly on the ground
Yet he fears neither wind nor sun—
It's only in floods he has no fun.

兩頭尖尖像貌丑

終年只在地裏走

烈日刮風都不怕

就怕火水浸滿頭

earthworm

A mouth like two clappers,
Two small fans for feet,
He's slow upon land
But in water is fleet.

嘴像小鏟子　脚像小扇子

走路晃膀子　水上划船子

duck

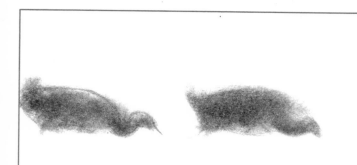

This weird bridge is addling
my mind—look! it's paddling
with two pairs of odd little oars!
This green stone is slip-
ping and making me trip.
Oh! I think that I'll go back indoors!

青石板滑石橋
四把槳慢慢搖

turtle

In summer, in his suit of green,
He catches insects on the wing.
The north wind blows him off the scene
But he'll be in the swim, come spring.

身穿綠袍小英雄
夏天田裏捉害蟲
北風一吹不見了
春天又在池塘中

frog

They're small in size, but never mind,
They're very strong, as you will find.
They function very well in teams
And really love to work, it seems.

別看身體小　力量可不小
有時搬糧食　有時挖地道
大家能團結　個個愛勤勞

ant

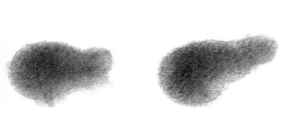

This old man's back is bent in half,
His tousled whiskers make us laugh.
He sheds no blood, but when he's dead
His body turns a brilliant red.

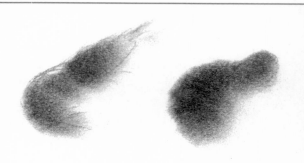

駄背老公公鬍子亂蓬蓬

身前沒有血死後滿身紅

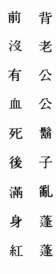

shrimp

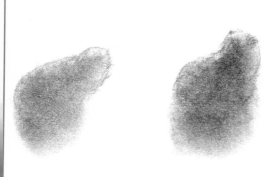

With fur his body's covered up;
Sometimes he looks just like a pup.
Instead of feet he has four hands,
Yet very like a man he stands.

一身毛四只手
站着坐着像個人
伏着爬着像個狗

monkey

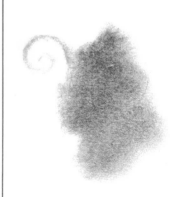

Just two hairs grow upon her head,
But she wears a flowered gown
And dances along the flower bed—
The prettiest creature in town!

頭上兩根毛身穿花旗袍
飛午花叢中快樂又消遙

butterfly

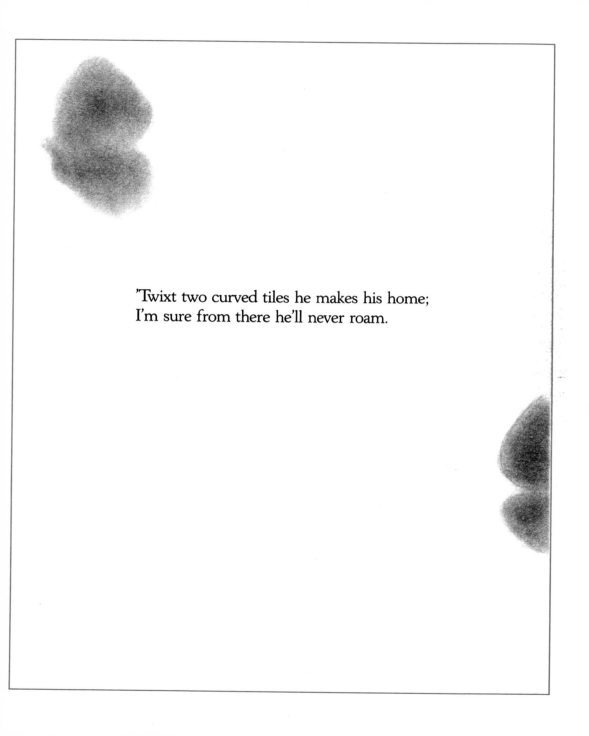

'Twixt two curved tiles he makes his home;
I'm sure from there he'll never roam.

兩張瓦片蓋個房間
一位胖子住在裏邊

clam

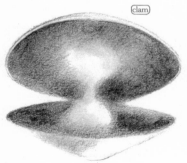

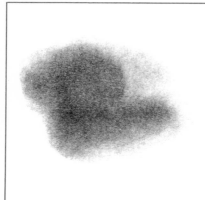

He lives like a monkey;
He's built like a mouse.
He picks nuts and fruits
In his tree-branch house.

形狀像老鼠
生活像猴子
爬在樹枝上
忙着採果子

squirrel

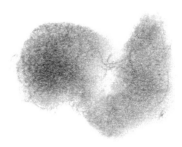

His costume is splendid, all golden and red
And he wears a red flower on top of his head.
You can see he's the boss here, for one and all
Come out when they hear his morning call.

頭戴大紅花身穿金紅褂
好像當家人早起喚人家

rooster

He has no neck, but has a head;
He lives, yet is as cold as dead.
A journey of a thousand miles
He travels, though no feet has he,
Nor can he fly, though he has wings.
What kind of creature can he be?

有頭沒有頸有氣冷冰冰

有翅不能飛沒腳千里行

(fish)

Though he gets a new coat about four times a month
He feels not a smidgeon of guilt
For his labor's for others to gain, not himself
And he works till his house is all built.

生來人家稱寶寶
一月四次換外套
辛勤工作爲人忙
盖好房子就睡覺

silkworm

This long-legged rascal, coming
sneaking into your bedroom, humming
as he helps himself to your best red
wine ... CLAP your hands, and he's dead!

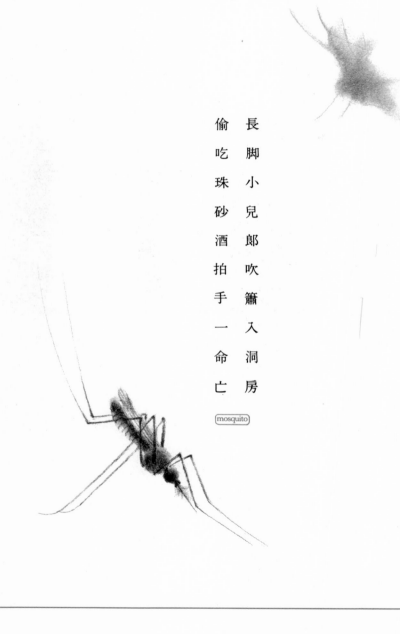

長腳小兒郎吹簫入洞房
偷吃珠砂酒拍手一命亡

mosquito

He walks about on silent feet,
Seeking the fish he loves to eat.
To sleep all day he thinks is right;
He does his hunting in the night.

脚穿釘鞋走天聲

不吃素菜吃魚腥

日日無事打瞌睡

半夜三更尋點心

cat

His suit looks so torn
As he soars in the sky,
But don't waste your pity on him.
See his mouth like a hook
When he steals little chicks—
He's a bandit and killer quite grim.

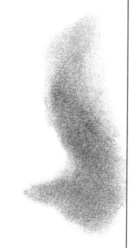

身穿破簑衣飛在半空裏
嘴巴像鈎子常常偷小鷄

hawk

This dandy wears a coat of black
With handsome scissor-tails in back.
He winters in the south, and then
He comes north in the spring again.

身披黑緞袍尾巴像剪刀

冬天向南去春暖回來早

swallow

High on a hill grows a neat patch of grass.
How many separate blades? No one can guess.

High on a ridge they grow,
Not too thin,
Not too thick,
Each one is a perfect row.

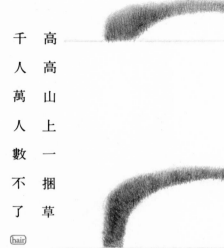

千　高
人　高
萬　山
人　上
數　一
不　捆
了　草

(hair)

不　高
稀　高
不　山
密　上
剛　種
兩　韮
排　菜

(eyebrows)

Two windows which are way up high
Face north, south, east and west.
Opening them lets in no air,
But light shines through them best.

Out of the plain
Rises a hill.
Your feet can't reach its crest,
Try as they will.
Both hands can touch it;
One eye can view it;
But, though they try their best,
Two eyes can't do it.

高樓兩只窗東西南北望
開窗不透氣照見一片亮

eyes

平地一高山
兩眼看不見
手可摸到山頂
脚踏不到山邊

nose

Inside a red cave
A strange bridge you'll see.
One end is tied down
Yet the other moves free.

Roots above,
Stems below,
Though watered daily
No flowers grow.

紅石洞裏一座橋
一頭生根一頭搖

tongue

根在上
葉在下
天天澆水
永不開花

beard

About Ed Young

Speaking of his work as an illustrator, Ed Young has said:

A unique spirit reigns in the heart of every story. It is the task of the illustrator to become like a blank sheet of paper in order to win it. Once touched, he must allow that spark to kindle and give play to every visual expression within his means until the inspiration matures and gathers into a form of its own choosing. This form in turn, enriches the illustration and all who might come across it.

Born in Tientsin, China, Ed Young grew up in Shanghai and came to the United States in his late teens. He studied architecture at the University of Illinois, but a summer of study at the Art Center in Los Angeles convinced him that his real interest was in the field of graphic art and illustration, and he transferred to the Art Center for several more years of study and a degree in Fine Arts. He now lives in a suburb of New York City.

Among the many beautiful books Mr. Young has illustrated are THE EMPEROR AND THE KITE, a Caldecott Honor Book (written by Jane Yolen), the pictures for which are created in colored papercuts; THE ROOSTER'S HORNS, a shadow puppet play which tells in words and pictures how children can enjoy and perform this traditional Chinese craft in their own homes; and THE TERRIBLE NUNG GWAMA, which grew out of his desire to bring the robust spirit and wit, as well as the beauty of Chinese folktales to young people in this country. Now, with HIGH ON A HILL: A Book of Chinese Riddles, he shares yet another delightful aspect of Chinese folklore with Western readers. The pictures in HIGH ON A HILL were executed in pencil on paper. Each of these books is illustrated in a different manner and technique, representing in Ed Young's own highly individual way the variety and charm of traditional Oriental art styles.

Library of Congress Cataloging in Publication Data
Young, Ed.   High on a hill.
SUMMARY: A collection of riddles translated
from the Chinese.
1. Riddles, Chinese — Juvenile literature.
[1. Riddles] I. Title.
PN6371.5.Y6   398.6   79-24070
ISBN 0-529-05553-8T
ISBN 0-529-05554-6 R